Franklin Productions Ltd in association with Ground Rush Productions and Neil McPherson for the Finborough Theatre presents

T0353298

The World Premiere

THE SOFT OF HER PALM

by Chris Dunkley

Supported using public funding by

ARTS COUNCIL ENGLAND

LOTTERY FUNDED

FINBOROUGH | THEATRE

First performed at the Finborough Theatre as a staged reading as part of *Vibrant - An Anniversary Festival of Finborough Playwrights*: Friday, 4 June 2010.
First performance at the Finborough Theatre: Sunday, 7 October 2012

THE SOFT OF HER PALM

by Chris Dunkley

Cast in order of speaking

Sarah	**Tilly Gaunt**
Phil	**Simon Bubb**
Poppy	**Abigail Cole Jarvie**
Poppy	**Carmelina Meoli**
Lucy	**Siubhan Harrison**
Mick	**Sean Murray**

The play takes place in Northampton and moves backwards in time between 2012 and 2011.

The performance lasts approximately ninety minutes.

There will be no interval.

Director	**Ola Ince**
Designer	**Daniel Harvey**
Lighting Designer	**Elliot Griggs**
Sound Designer	**Max Pappenheim**
Movement Director	**Jenny Ogilvie**
Fight Director	**Kevin McCurdy**
Stage Manager	**Ben Karakashian**
Assistant Director	**Suzanne West**
Producer	**Georgina Ratnatunga** for **Franklin Productions Ltd**
Associate Producer	**Alan Sharpington** for **Ground Rush Productions**

Our patrons are respectfully reminded that, in this intimate theatre, any noise such as rustling programmes, talking or the ringing of mobile phones may distract the actors and your fellow audience-members.

We regret there is no admittance or re-admittance to the auditorium whilst the performance is in progress.

The Soft of Her Palm is performed in repertoire and on the set of *A Life*, designed by James Turner, which plays Tuesday to Saturday evenings, and Saturday and Sunday matinees, until 27 October 2012.

Simon Bubb | Phil
Trained at the Webber Douglas Academy of Dramatic Art.
Theatre includes *The Habit of Art*, *War Horse* and *Saint Joan* (National Theatre), *Romeo and Juliet*, *Much Ado About Nothing* and *King John* (Royal Shakespeare Company), *The Philanthropist* (Donmar Warehouse), *24 Hour Plays* (Old Vic New Voices), *Hay Fever* (Royal Exchange Theatre, Manchester), *Unless* (Stephen Joseph Theatre, Scarborough), *Stealing Sweets and Punching People* (Theatre503) and *The Edge of the Land* (Eastern Angles).
Television includes *EastEnders*.
Radio includes *The Archers*, *Clare in the Community*, *A Tale of Two Cities*, *My One and Only*, *Pilgrim*, *Blurred*, *Life and Fate*, *The Haunted Hotel*, *The Spy*, *Disconnected* and *Nightingale Wood*.

Tilly Gaunt | Sarah
Trained at Bristol Old Vic Theatre School.
Theatre includes *Translations* (Curve Theatre, Leicester), *The Yellow Wallpaper* (Royal Festival Hall), *The Count of Monte Cristo* (West Yorkshire Playhouse), *Peter Pan*, *A Doll's House* and *Ruby Moon* (Northern Stage, Newcastle), *Noises Off* (National Theatre Tour and Piccadilly Theatre), *Charley's Aunt* (National Tour for Bill Kenwright Ltd), *Twelfth Night* (Nuffield Theatre, Southampton), *The Memory of Water* (Nuffield Theatre, Southampton and Guildford), *The Real Thing*, *Lovers* and *War* (Strindberg Intima Theatre, Stockholm) and *Silence* (National Theatre Studio).
Television includes several episodes of *Holby City*, *The South Bank Show*, *The Bill*, *People Like Us* and the BBC comedy *Moonmonkeys*.
For Radio, Tilly won the Carleton Hobbs Radio Award and has performed in over one hundred radio productions.

Siubhan Harrison | Lucy
At the Finborough Theatre, Siubhan appeared in *In Quest of Conscience* (2011).
Trained at the Guildford School of Acting.
Theatre includes *Earthquakes in London* (National Tour and National Theatre for Headlong), *Rich Isn't Easy* (Tristan Bates Theatre), *Grease* (Piccadilly Theatre), *The Stripper* (National Tour), *Marguerite* (Theatre Royal Haymarket), *Marianne Dreams* (Almeida Theatre), *We Will Rock You* (Dominion Theatre), *Bad Girls the Musical* (West Yorkshire Playhouse), *Les Misérables* (Queen's Theatre), *Carmen* (New Vic and Regional Tour) *Castaway Café* (Edinburgh Festival), *Whale Music* (Medena Theatre) and a special concert version of *Les Misérables* performed at Windsor Castle for the Entente Cordiale.
Film includes the Cannes-nominated film *The Man Who Met Himself*, *Well Prepared* and *Little Deaths* which opened the Glasgow Fright Fest last year.
Television includes *Al Murray's Happy Hour*, *Saturday Night Takeaway*, *This Morning*, *The Alan Titchmarsh Show* and *The Song of Lunch*.

Abigail Cole Jarvie | Poppy
Abigail trains at Phoenix Theatre School.
Theatre includes *Annie*, *Christmas Production* and *Fairytale Mashup!* (Phoenix Theatre School).

Carmelina Meoli | Poppy
Carmelina trains at Stagecoach Fulham and is part of the street dance group at GEMS Hampshire School. She has previously trained at Chelsea Ballet School and Dance Attic Ballet. Theatre includes *On the Roof* and a number of open-air performances for Stagecoach Fulham.

Sean Murray | Mick

At the Finborough Theatre, Sean appeared in *Death of Long Pig* (2009).

Other theatre includes *The Tempest* (Theatre Royal, Bath), *Kes* (Catherine Wheels Theatre), *Romeo and Juliet* and The *Importance of Being Earnest* (Royal Lyceum Theatre, Edinburgh), The *English Game* (Headlong), *The Home Place* (Comedy Theatre), *Buried Child* (National Theatre), *Jane Eyre* (Shared Experience), *The Crucible* (The Touring Consortium), *The Terrible Voice of Satan* (Royal Court Theatre), *The Cherry Orchard*, *The Phoenician Women*, *The Virtuoso*, *Two Gentlemen of Verona*, *Romeo and Juliet*, *A Woman Killed with Kindness* and *Amphibians* (Royal Shakespeare Company), *The Fairy Queen* (Aix-en-Provence), *Androcles and the Lion*, *Judy*, *Tartuffe*, *The Life of Galileo*, *The School for Scandal*, *The Rivals*, *The Comedy of Errors* and *Othello* (Bristol Old Vic Theatre), *For King and Country* (Greenwich Theatre), *The Misanthrope* (Cambridge Theatre Company), *Loot* (Mercury Theatre, Colchester), *One Flew over the Cuckoo's Nest* and *Peter Pan* (Redgrave Theatre, Farnham) and *Murder on the Nile* (Worthing Theatre).

Film includes *The Truth*, *Finding Mallory*, *A Rather English Marriage* and *Hamlet*.

Television includes *Robin Hood*, *Casualty*, *Judge John Deed*, *Dunkirk*, *Holby City*, *Serious and Organised*, *Silent Witness*, *Without Motive*, *Berkeley Square*, *Seaforth*, *The Bill*, *The March*, *A Wing and a Prayer*, *Peak Practice*, *Smokescreen*, *The Advocates*, *South of the Border*, *The Country Boy* and *EastEnders*.

Chris Dunkley | Playwright
Chris is currently commissioned by the Arts Council to research
and write *The Precariat*, a new play that will premiere as part
of the Finborough Theatre's *Vibrant – A Festival of Finborough
Playwrights* in November 2012. His play *Mirita* premiered at
the Finborough Theatre in 2001, was named *Time Out* Critics'
Choice, and transferred Off Broadway to the Cherry Lane
Theatre, New York City, alongside his short play *Lisa Says*. An
earlier version *of The Soft of Her Palm* was performed at the
Finborough Theatre as a staged reading as part of *Vibrant – An
Anniversary Festival of Finborough Playwrights* (2010), directed
by Tim Luscombe.
Other plays include *Almost Blue* (Riverside Studios), *How to
Tell the Truth* (Stephen Joseph Theatre, Scarborough), *Lucy is
a Minger* (Spinney Hill Theatre, Northampton) and *The Festival*
(Wimbledon Studio Theatre). Radio includes *The All Colour
Vegetarian Cookbook* and *The Architects*, both for the BBC.
Chris has been Writer in Residence at Royal and Derngate
Theatres, Northampton, and Writer on Attachment at the Royal
Court Theatre. He was the 2002 winner of the International
Student Playscript Competition and winner of the PMA writers'
award in 2001.

Ola Ince | Director
Ola is a former Resident Assistant Director and Senior Reader
at the Finborough Theatre where she directed *Namaskar* as
part of 2011's *Vibrant – A Festival of Finborough Playwrights*.
Trained at Rose Bruford College with a First Class Honours BA
in Theatre Directing. Directing includes *Pets Corner* (Arcola
Theatre), *One Million Tiny Plays About Britain* (Clare Theatre
at The Young Vic), *Games* (Pleasance Theatre), *Far Away* (The
Studio, Rose Bruford College), *The Inconvenient Store* (Tooting
Hub), *The Frame* (Unicorn Theatre), *The Island* (Unicorn
Theatre) and *Pop* (Warehouse Theatre). Ola has worked as
an Assistant Director for the The Young Vic, Octagon Theatre
Bolton, Tristan Bates Theatre, National Theatre Studio, King's
Head Theatre and the Royal Shakespeare Company Fringe
Festival. Most recently, she was Assistant Director to Sacha
Wares on *Wild Swans* (The Young Vic).

Daniel Harvey | Designer
Trained at the Victorian College of the Arts, Melbourne.
Set Designs include *Hedda Gabler* (The International Ibsen
Stage at Hoxton Hall), *O Brave New World* – based on *The*

Tempest (Retz London). Costume Designs include the Australian premiere of *Xanadu: The Musical* (Australian Tour). Set and Costume Designs include *Back from the Dead Red*, which received a nominated for Best Design in the Green Room Awards (Melbourne Fringe Festival), *Two Weeks with the Queen* (Black Apple Theatre at the Midsumma Festival). Daniel has worked as Assistant to Paul Wills on *My Fair Lady* (Sheffield Crucible), *Drumbelly* (Abbey Theatre, Dublin), as Assistant to Chloe Lamford on *Disco Pigs* (The Young Vic), *Salt, Root and Roe* (Donmar Warehouse at Trafalgar Studios), *An Appointment with the Wickerman* (National Theatre of Scotland), *Boys* (Headlong at Soho Theatre) and *The Little Sweep* (Malmo Opera House), as Assistant to Christopher Oram on *Uncle Vanya* (Vaudeville Theatre), *Privates on Parade* (Noël Coward Theatre) and *The Marriage of Figaro* (Glyndebourne Festival Opera) and as Assistant to Anna Tregloan on the Australian premiere of *Spring Awakening: A New Musical* (Sydney Theatre Company). Wardrobe includes *Priscilla – Queen of the Desert: The Musical* (Palace Theatre) and the Melbourne seasons for both The Australian Ballet and Opera Australia.

Elliot Griggs | Lighting Designer
At the Finborough Theatre, Elliot has been the Lighting Designer for *Crush* (2011), *Perchance to Dream* (2011), *Portraits* (2011), *And I and Silence* (2011) and *Northern Star* (2011).
Trained at the Royal Academy of Dramatic Art. Recent theatre includes *The Boy Who Kicked Pigs* (The Lowry, Manchester), *MEAT* (Theatre503), *Belleville Rendez-Vous* (Greenwich Theatre), *Lagan* (Oval House Theatre), *Folk Contraption* (Southbank Centre), *Bitter Pleasures for a Sour Generation* (Soho Theatre), *The Custard Boys* (Tabard Theatre), *Brightest and Best* (Half Moon Theatre), *Dealing With Clair*, *One Minute*, *Nocturnal*, *dirty butterfly*, *Our Town* (Royal Academy of Dramatic Art), *The Mercy Seat* (Royal Shakespeare Company Capital Centre, Warwick), *The Lady's Not For Burning*, *West Side Story*, *By the Bog of Cats*, *'Tis Pity She's a Whore*, *Elephant's Graveyard* (Warwick Arts Centre), *Much Ado About Nothing* (Belgrade Theatre, Coventry) and *Dido and Aeneas* (St. Paul's Church, London, and Tour). His awards for lighting design include the Francis Reid Award from the Association of Lighting Designers and the ShowLight Award at the National Student Drama Festival.

Max Pappenheim | Sound Designer
At the Finborough Theatre, Max designed the sound for *Hindle Wakes*, *Barrow Hill* and *The Fear of Breathing* (2012) and directed *Perchance to Dream* (2011).
Sound Designs include *Borderland*, *Kafka v Kafka* (Brockley Jack Studio Theatre), *Being Tommy Cooper* (Old Red Lion Theatre), *Four Corners One Heart* (Theatre503), *Tangent* (New Diorama Theatre) and *Werther's Sorrows* and *Salome* (Edinburgh Festival and Etcetera Theatre). Directing includes *San Giuda* (Southwark Cathedral), *The Charmed Life* (King's Head Theatre), *Finchley Road* (LOST Theatre) and *Quid Pro Quo* (Riverside Studios).
Max was nominated for an OffWestEnd Award 2012 for Best Sound Design.

Jenny Ogilvie | Movement Director
At the Finborough Theatre, Jenny appeared in *Wolfboy/Treatment* (1999) and *Beating Heart Cadaver* as part of *Vibrant – A Festival of Finborough Playwrights* (2010).
Trained as an actress at the Webber Douglas Academy of Dramatic Art and as a Movement Director at the Central School of Speech and Drama. Movement Direction includes *Sweeney Todd* and *Paul Bunyan* workshops (Welsh National Opera), *Vernon God Little* (Guildford School of Acting), *Three Sisters/Swan Song*, which she co-directed with Ben Naylor, *Richard III* and *Antony and Cleopatra* (Central School of Speech and Drama). As an actor, theatre includes *What Every Woman Knows* (Royal Exchange Theatre, Manchester) for which she was nominated for the TMA Award for Best Performance in a Play, *Noughts and Crosses* (Royal Shakespeare Company), *I Have Been Here Before* (Watford Palace Theatre), *Peter Pan* and *The Diary of Anne Frank* (Birmingham Rep and National Tour), *Our Country's Good* (National Tour), *Rebecca* and *Deadlock* (Vienna's English Theatre) and *Miss Julie* (Theatre Royal, Haymarket). Film includes *A Cock and Bull Story* and *The Clap.* Television includes *Law and Order*, *Torn*, *Five Days* and *Poirot*.

Kevin McCurdy | Fight Director
Trained at The Royal Welsh College of Music and Drama and is an Equity professional First Director in Wales. He gained his Combat Teacher status in 1993 and Professional Fight Directors status in 1996. Theatre includes *Mogadishu* (Royal Exchange Theatre, Manchester, and National Tour), *Romeo and*

Juliet (Nuffield Theatre, Southampton), *The Three Musketeers* (Cardiff Castle), *Of Mice and Men*, *The Grapes of Wrath* (Clwyd Theatr Cymru), *House and Garden*, *Things We Do For Love*, *Sleeping Beauty*, *Dick Whittington* (Harrogate Theatre), *Taboo* (National Tour), *Maid Marian and Her Merry Men*, *The Birthday Party*, *It's Not The End Of The World*, *Suspension*, *Cyrano De Bergerac* (Bristol Old Vic), *Beauty and The Beast* (Sherman Theatre, Cardiff), *Quadrophenia* (Sherman Theatre, Cardiff), *Cysgod Y Cryman* (Theatr Genedlaethol), *We The People*, *The Frontline*, *As You Like It*, *Troilus and Cressida*, *Bedlam*, *Helen*, *Macbeth* (Shakespeare's Globe), *Treasure Island* (Rose Theatre, Kingston), *Cause Célèbre* (The Old Vic),*The Heart of Robin Hood*, *Twelfth Night*, *Marat Sade*, *The Comedy of Errors*, *The Tempest*, *Much Ado About Nothing* and *Julius Caesar* (Royal Shakespeare Company). Feature Films include *John Carter of Mars*, *Season of the Witch*, *Hunky Dory*, *Panic Button*, *Flick*, *Summer Scars* and *A World Apart*. Film and Television includes *The Chosen*, *Doctor Who Christmas Special*, *Torchwood*, *Becoming Human*, *Belonging*, *Being Human*, *High Hopes*, *The Story of Tracy Beaker*, *Hearts of Gold*, *Carrie's War*, *Pobol Y Cwm*, *Rhyw a Dinosaurs*, *Jara*, *Y Pris*, *Caerdydd*, *Pen Taler*, *Gwaith Cyntaf*, *Alys*, *CCTV*, *Camelot*, *Baker Boys*, *Switch*, *Hollyoaks After Dark*, *Arthurs' Dyke* and *Arwyr* and *Colonial Gods*. Opera includes *Wozzeck*, *Die Fledermaus*, *Rigoletto*, *Tristan Und Isolde*, *Don Giovanni* (Welsh National Opera) and *The Cunning Little Vixen* (Glyndebourne Opera). Kevin has been Resident Fight Master at the Royal Welsh Colleges' since 2005.

Ben Karakashian | Stage Manager
At the Finborough Theatre, Ben was Stage Manager on *Perchance to Dream* (2011), *The Grand Duke* (2012) and *Hindle Wakes* (2012).
Trained at Royal Holloway University of London with BA Honours in Drama and Theatre Studies. Stage Management includes *The Folk Contraption* (Old Vic Tunnels), *Someone to Blame* (King's Head Theatre), *The Mikado* (Rosemary Branch Theatre and King's Head Theatre), *Susanna's Secret* (King's Head Theatre) and *Beowulf: The Panto* (Rosemary Branch Theatre).

Suzanne West | Assistant Director
Trained as an actor at the Royal Academy of Dramatic Art and recently completed an MA in Contemporary Performance Making at Brunel University. As an actor, performances include

The School for Scandal (Harrogate Theatre), *On The Piste* (Harrogate Theatre) and *Hamlet* (Theatre Du Jour, Argen, France as part of the International Theatre Festival). As a director, she is currently developing *Losing It* with writer Fran Perillo for a tour in 2013.

Georgina Ratnatunga for Franklin Productions Ltd |
Producer
At the Finborough Theatre, Georgina was formerly General Manager. She was Producer for *Portraits* (2011), Associate Producer for *Perchance to Dream* (2011) and – for Franklin Productions Ltd – she produced *The American Clock* (2012). Franklin Productions Ltd was formed in 2010 to produce plays and musicals in London, touring the UK and internationally.
Producer | **Neil Franklin**
Associate Producer | **Georgina Ratnatunga**
www.franklinproductions.co.uk

Alan Sharpington for Ground Rush Productions | Associate Producer
Alan's producing and directing work includes *The Dark Entry* (Canterbury Festival), *The Yellow Wallpaper* (Royal Festival Hall) and *The Case* (Oubliette Arthouse), all in site-specific productions for Donkeywork where he is Co-Artistic Director, *Romeo and Juliet* (New Zealand Tour), *Tales of the Black Hand* (Tricycle Theatre) and *The Wake* (Soho Theatre Studio). As an actor, he has worked at the Tricycle Theatre, the Orange Tree Theatre, Richmond, Soho Theatre Studio, Arcola Theatre and many tours and site-specific shows. Ground Rush Productions was founded to produce the very best in new writing and to revive neglected classics.

Production Acknowledgements
Chaperones | **Kidist Admasu, Sarah Jarvie, Carmine Meoli**
Assistant Stage Manager | **Ine De Baerdemaeker**
Operator | **Anna Braybrooke**
Production Image | **David Armstrong**

Thanks to
Rob Crouch, Marian Elizabeth, Nabil Elouahabi, Emily Lim, Charlotte Mafham, Claire Owens, Julia Stenton, Ros Terry, Islington Community Theatre, and the Princess Victoria, Shepherd's Bush.

FINBOROUGH | THEATRE

Winner – Eight awards at the OffWestEnd Awards 2012

"A theatre in a class of its own: last year's programme was so good that it was worth moving to West Brompton for...Its first new writing premiere of the year...suggests that 2012 in London's only wine bar theatre, will be as impressive as it was in 2011." *Time Out*

"A disproportionately valuable component of the London theatre ecology. Its programme combines new writing and revivals, in selections intelligent and audacious." *Financial Times*

"A blazing beacon of intelligent endeavour, nurturing new writers while finding and reviving neglected curiosities from home and abroad." *The Daily Telegraph*

Founded in 1980, the multi-award-winning Finborough Theatre presents plays and music theatre, concentrated exclusively on new writing and genuine rediscoveries from the 19th and 20th centuries. We aim to offer a stimulating and inclusive programme, appealing to theatregoers of all ages and from a broad spectrum of the population. Behind the scenes, we continue to discover and develop a new generation of theatre makers – through our vibrant Literary team, our internship programme, our Resident Assistant Director Programme, and our partnership with the National Theatre Studio providing a bursary for Emerging Directors.

Despite remaining completely unsubsidised, the Finborough Theatre has an unparalleled track record of attracting the finest creative talent, as well as discovering new playwrights who go on to become leading voices in British theatre. Under

Artistic Director Neil McPherson, it has discovered some of the UK's most exciting new playwrights including Laura Wade, James Graham, Mike Bartlett, Sarah Grochala, Jack Thorne, Simon Vinnicombe, Alexandra Wood, Al Smith, Nicholas de Jongh and Anders Lustgarten.

Artists working at the theatre in the 1980s included Clive Barker, Rory Bremner, Nica Burns, Kathy Burke, Ken Campbell, Jane Horrocks and Claire Dowie. In the 1990s, the Finborough Theatre became known for new writing including Naomi Wallace's first play *The War Boys*; Rachel Weisz in David Farr's *Neville Southall's Washbag*; four plays by Anthony Neilson including *Penetrator* and *The Censor*, both of which transferred to the Royal Court Theatre; and new plays by Richard Bean, Lucinda Coxon, David Eldridge, Tony Marchant, Mark Ravenhill and Phil Willmott. New writing development included a number of works that went on to become modern classics including Mark Ravenhill's *Shopping and F***king*, Conor McPherson's *This Lime Tree Bower*, Naomi Wallace's *Slaughter City* and Martin McDonagh's *The Pillowman.*

Since 2000, new British plays have included Laura Wade's London debut *Young Emma*, commissioned for the Finborough Theatre; James Graham's *Albert's Boy* with Victor Spinetti; Sarah Grochala's *S27*; Peter Nichols' *Lingua Franca*, which transferred Off-Broadway; and West End transfers for Joy Wilkinson's *Fair*; Nicholas de Jongh's *Plague Over England*; and Jack Thorne's *Fanny and Faggot*. The late Miriam Karlin made her last stage appearance in *Many Roads to Paradise* in 2008. Many of the Finborough Theatre's new plays have been published and are on sale from our website.

UK premieres of foreign plays have included Brad Fraser's *Wolfboy*; Lanford Wilson's *Sympathetic Magic*; Larry Kramer's *The Destiny of Me*; Tennessee Williams' *Something Cloudy, Something Clear*; the English premiere of Robert McLellan's Scots language classic, *Jamie the Saxt*; and three West End transfers – Frank McGuinness' *Gates of Gold* with William Gaunt and John Bennett, Joe DiPietro's *F***ing Men* and Craig Higginson's *Dream of the Dog* with Dame Janet Suzman.

Rediscoveries of neglected work have included the first London revivals of Rolf Hochhuth's *Soldiers* and *The Representative*; both parts of Keith Dewhurst's *Lark Rise to Candleford*; *The Women's War*, an evening of original suffragette plays; *Etta Jenks* with Clarke Peters and Daniela Nardini; Noël Coward's first play, *The Rat Trap*; Charles Wood's *Jingo* with Susannah Harker; Emlyn Williams' *Accolade* with Aden Gillett and Graham Seed; and Lennox Robinson's *Drama at Inish* with Celia Imrie and Paul O'Grady.

Music Theatre has included the new (premieres from Grant Olding, Charles Miller, Michael John LaChuisa, Adam Guettel, Andrew Lippa and Adam Gwon's *Ordinary Days* which transferred to the West End) and the old (the UK premiere of Rodgers and Hammerstein's *State Fair* which also transferred to the West End, and the acclaimed Celebrating British Music Theatre series, reviving forgotten British musicals including *Gay's The Word* by Ivor Novello with Sophie-Louise Dann, Helena Blackman and Elizabeth Seal.

The Finborough Theatre won *The Stage* Fringe Theatre of the Year Award in 2011, won *London Theatre Reviews'* Empty Space Peter Brook Award in 2010, the Empty Space Peter Brook Award's Dan Crawford Pub Theatre Award in 2005 and 2008, the Empty Space Peter Brook Mark Marvin Award in 2004, four awards in the inaugural 2011 OffWestEnd Awards and swept the board with eight awards at the 2012 OffWestEnd Awards including Best Artistic Director and Best Director for the second year running. *Accolade* was named Best Fringe Show of 2011 by *Time Out*. It is the only unsubsidised theatre to be awarded the Pearson Playwriting Award bursary for writers Chris Lee in 2000, Laura Wade in 2005 for James Graham in 2006, for Al Smith in 2007, for Anders Lustgarten in 2009, Simon Vinnicombe in 2010 and Dawn King in 2011. Three bursary holders (Laura Wade, James Graham and Anders Lustgarten) have also won the Catherine Johnson Award for Pearson Best Play.

www.finboroughtheatre.co.uk

The Associate Director position is supported by The National Theatre Studio's Bursary for Emerging Directors, a partnership between the National Theatre Studio and the Finborough Theatre.

The Finborough Theatre has the support of the Pearson Playwrights' Scheme. Sponsored by Pearson PLC.

The Cameron Mackintosh Resident Composer Scheme is facilitated by Mercury Musical Developments and Musical Theatre Matters

The Finborough Theatre is a member of the Independent Theatre Council, Musical Theatre Network UK and The Earl's Court Society www.earlscourtsociety.org.uk

The Finborough Wine Café
Contact Monique Ziervogel on 020 7373 0745 or finboroughwinecafe@gmail.com

Mailing
Email admin@finboroughtheatre.co.uk or give your details to our Box Office staff to join our free email list. If you would like to be sent a free season leaflet every three months, just include your postal address and postcode.

Follow Us Online

 www.facebook.com/FinboroughTheatre
www.twitter.com/finborough

Feedback
We welcome your comments, complaints and suggestions. Write to Finborough Theatre, 118 Finborough Road, London SW10 9ED or email us at admin@finboroughtheatre.co.uk

Friends

The Finborough Theatre is a registered charity. We receive no public funding, and rely solely on the support of our audiences. Please do consider supporting us by becoming a member of our Friends of the Finborough Theatre scheme. There are four categories of Friends, each offering a wide range of benefits

Brandon Thomas Friends – Bruce Cleave. Matthew Littleford. Sean W. Swalwell. Michael Rangos.

Richard Tauber Friends – Neil Dalrymple. Richard Jackson. M. Kramer. Harry MacAuslan. Brian Smith. Mike Lewendon.

William Terriss Friends – Leo and Janet Liebster. Peter Lobl. Bhags Sharma. Thurloe and Lyndhurst LLP. Jon Sedmak. Jan Topham.

Smoking is not permitted in the auditorium and the use of cameras and recording equipment is strictly prohibited

THE SOFT OF HER PALM

Chris Dunkley

THE SOFT OF HER PALM

OBERON BOOKS
LONDON

WWW.OBERONBOOKS.COM

First published in 2012 by Oberon Books Ltd
521 Caledonian Road, London N7 9RH
Tel: +44 (0) 20 7607 3637 / Fax: +44 (0) 20 7607 3629
e-mail: info@oberonbooks.com

A catalogue record for this book is available from the British
Library.

PB ISBN: 978-1-84943-393-8
E ISBN: 978-1-84943-728-8

Cover design by Matt Watkins

eBook conversion
by CPI Group (UK) Ltd, Croydon, CR0 4YY.

For Sonya

Characters

PHIL – early 30s

LUCY – early 30s

SARAH – early 30s

POPPY – 7

MICK – 50s

This play was developed with support from Arts Council England and The Peggy Ramsay Foundation.

PHIL stares at SARAH from the middle of the living room. The front door is open to the street; SARAH is inside, but only just.

SARAH: She was screaming. We must have been… ten feet away from each other… his wife was screaming at him… and he just stared at me… this stranger… staring at each other.

PHIL doesn't answer.

But he sat there with steam… or something… something coming out of his engine… all his life just hissing out in front of me… and I thought 'how dare you?' you know?… How dare you interrupt my day with this little picture of death… ?

PHIL: Was anyone hurt?

SARAH: I need a drink.

Pause.

PHIL: So he didn't die? The man in the car. You said death.

SARAH: He looked like he just wanted to rest his head on the steering wheel and fall asleep.

She exits to the kitchen.

PHIL: And you're okay.

SARAH: *(Off.)* What?

She re-enters.

PHIL: I mean it was a non-fatal crash.

SARAH: Phil, what're you

PHIL: You crashed your car on the way here. Into another car. And everyone's still alive. The man, his wife and you. Is your car all right?

SARAH: Just drop it. Leave it. I can never tell when you're taking the piss. You know I hate that. And why did you move the fridge?

PHIL: I think the point is… I think the point I'm making is that I didn't invite you in. I mean, perhaps you shouldn't be in here. I mean definitely.

She stares at him. Pause. She goes back to the kitchen.

SARAH: *(Off.)* You look terrible.

Pause.

(Off.) Are you going to ask me how I've been?

PHIL: I know how you've been.

SARAH: *(Off.)* Do you?

PHIL: Yes.

SARAH: *(Entering with two glasses of wine.)* Do you really, Phil?

PHIL: Of course I do; you've been following me.

Pause.

SARAH: I shouldn't have come.

PHIL: You just got here.

SARAH: What am I thinking? I came to… not thinking straight.

PHIL: I haven't said anything.

Pause.

SARAH: The wine's wrong.

PHIL: Okay. No wine.

SARAH: You have some.

PHIL: You don't live here.

SARAH: It's just I want to have a clear head. Besides, I'm driving… Jesus, what was I thinking?

She leaves a glass with him and goes back to the kitchen. PHIL looks at the glass. A moment. PHIL grabs his glass and downs it in one. He grimaces a little. SARAH re-enters with a similar grimace on her face. They look at each other. Pause.

PHIL: Sarah, I want you to get out.

SARAH: That's a shame, Phil, really. Is that all you can think to say? You're not going to ask how my daughter is?

Pause.

You've got some of her books.

PHIL: So you *were* heading over here when you crashed; this isn't some coincidence.

SARAH: Steve wanted to come with me. Said you're dangerous these days.

PHIL: He said that, did he?

SARAH: I'm not saying anything, he just

PHIL: He said that. He volunteered that.

SARAH: Yes, he said you seem different.

PHIL: I haven't seen Steve since he took over the restaurant.

SARAH: It's his opinion.

PHIL: Is it? His opinion. His current opinion.

SARAH: That's how he is.

PHIL: You would know I suppose.

SARAH: About what? What would I know about?

PHIL: He's all hats and billboards these days, isn't he, Steve? He's all neon and table decorations. Isn't Steve all fixtures and cheeseboards? A solid number three.

SARAH: I don't know what that means, but I know you're being provocative. Deliberately, I think. I came for the *Harry Potters* for Poppy.

PHIL: We used to argue who would win a fight, Gandalf or Dumbledore. She said Gandalf would win. I asked why… turns out it was because Richard Harris died. She couldn't… see Michael Gambon as the new Dumbledore. That's why Gandalf is stronger. I mean, for fuck's sake, Sarah. She's seven years old, but she… she sees through things already. Like you. Like a blade.

SARAH: Is this some desperate attempt to stay in her life? You're not her father.

PHIL: No, it's funny how I was never her father but now I'm I'm I'm definitely definitely

SARAH: You're the one not answering your phone.

He fetches the books, but doesn't give them to her.

SARAH: She ran away from school yesterday. Couldn't find her for hours.

PHIL: Why are you telling me?

SARAH: She said she'd found a dead otter… and then she started crying.

Pause.

PHIL: She did a project about them at school. I helped her with the

SARAH: I know what you did and didn't do. Why do you never answer your phone to me?

PHIL: I keep staring at things. Looking out on the avenue, just staring at nothing. Sometimes I think I've been doing it for hours. And then it's Friday and I realise it wasn't hours it was days. Just falling away.

SARAH: I know you're upset

She moves towards him gently. He moves away instinctively.

PHIL: You know… technically… these are mine.

SARAH: I'm sorry?

PHIL: I bought them.

SARAH: Are you serious? Phil?

PHIL: I want my things back.

SARAH: I gave you everything

PHIL: My computer, my books… I did everything I was supposed to do. I paid for the dress, the venue, the the the

SARAH: You haven't paid the gas bill, Phil, this is the real world. You agreed.

PHIL: My clothes, my… I mean… fucking Oxfam… Why do you keep following me? What do you think's going to happen?

SARAH: Oh, Phil. I have to drive past this house to get to work, I don't follow you.

During PHIL's following speech, SARAH's veneer drops and she begins to speak over him, becoming increasingly emotional.

PHIL: Yes, that's why you crashed. I looked out of the window upstairs and you were parked there on Sandringham Close watching the house. You saw me in the window and you tried to drive away as quickly as you could, but you crashed into another car. Mr Walker, number twelve. He was pulling into the close, about to turn into his driveway. Mrs Walker was screaming at him. She's an evangelical Christian. Mr Walker doesn't enjoy religion;

SARAH: You can be so cruel, Phil. Have you got any idea what the last six months has been like for me? To miss you all the time and hate you and the desperation Phil the desperation of all of that and to know that you're just here only a five minute drive away and that all it would take is the right words and the right gesture and it would all go away I just want it to go away I just want to rewind it just a bit and have you next to me Phil

31

in fact I think he hates it. I think he thinks that Jesus can go to hell for all he cares. I think he uses gardening as a way of escaping from her incessant moralising. That's who you crashed into. Mr Walker. A real person. I even took a picture with my phone. This is how I think now, this is the kind of thing I think I should be doing because you're completely nuts and I don't know what you're going to do next. I have a picture. I finally have proof.

I promise it won't be the same again I promise I promise I promise if you'll please just stop it all I'll do it I'll do it I'll do it I'm just tired and all I need is something to keep going for to just feel it again the way it was and to not keep bleeding that's what it feels like Phil like I'm bleeding and I can't hold it in and the more I bleed the more tired I get and I can't keep going like this I can't and I can't see an end to anything Phil please just let's just get back together and everything will be all right I need need need it to be the way it was you fucking cunt it's not much for you to

PHIL punches her in the face. Pause. She looks up at him. He doesn't move. He is breathing heavily. Something approaching exhilaration.

SARAH: She's saying you made her cuddle you. Poppy. Yesterday. I know you saw her. She ran away from school to come and meet you. She's saying you touched her. Are you grooming my daughter, Phil?

PHIL: If you really believed that you'd be talking to the police, not me.

SARAH: I called them this morning; they're coming to arrest you.

Pause. She lowers her tone and approaches him, softly.

I can help you, Phil.

She is close to him now. She kisses him. He does not respond. She gives up. She moves towards the door, but stops. It has dawned on her.

SARAH: I crashed my car.

Long pause.

PHIL: I'll give you a lift.

SARAH: The police will be here soon.

SARAH goes. PHIL stands alone. POPPY moves into the space with a handful of stones.

AUTUMN 2012. THE PREVIOUS DAY.

A dead otter in front of POPPY.

PHIL: Poppy?

Pause. He moves closer to her.

You okay?

POPPY: This is where we used to come because we used to play football over there, or we used to play war. And we didn't go home for ages.

PHIL: Poppy, I need to talk to you

POPPY: And one time you were chasing me because I was Billy the Kid and you were… who was it again?

PHIL: The teachers called me.

POPPY: What's his name? What was your name?

PHIL: Pat Garratt.

POPPY: Pat Garratt and I was Billy the Kid and I ran down here and you couldn't find me and you got scared because it was getting dark. And I shot you twice without you knowing, but you didn't die.

PHIL: The school rang me by mistake to tell me you went missing. Must still have my mobile on their records. I thought I'd find you here.

POPPY: Can we go to the cinema?

PHIL: No-one knows where you are. They're worried. Why did you come here? This is our place. Did you want to talk to me?

POPPY: Mum says she can't afford it, but that's a lie.

PHIL: They said something about you kicking one of your friends.

POPPY: Can we, Phil? Can we go to the pictures?

PHIL: Some other time.

POPPY: When?

PHIL: When you're old enough to buy me a ticket; I'm skint.

POPPY: Teachers never blink. Sometimes I'll be at school for a whole day and I won't see any teacher blink. Not one.

PHIL: They're all on drugs.

POPPY: Are they?

PHIL: No! Jesus, no. Don't listen to me, Poppy.

Pause.

Do you think he had a name?

POPPY: *(Unimpressed.)* He's an otter.

Pause.

PHIL: Poppy, are you angry at me for leaving? Is that what this is all about?

POPPY: Do you think he minds?

PHIL: Sorry?

POPPY: Just being left here. Do you think he minds?

PHIL: It was his home.

POPPY: I'd be cold.

> *Pause.*

> I was going to throw stones at him. But then I decided not to.

> *Pause.*

> Jenny told a lie today. Mrs Sladen said she shouldn't lie because of the boy and the wolf.

PHIL: Mrs Sladen's right.

POPPY: And I told Jenny she was a liar so she kicked me. I kicked her back. She did two things wrong and I'd done one thing right. They won't believe me. They always believe her. Can you come with me?

PHIL: I'm not allowed.

POPPY: Please.

PHIL: No-one's allowed to know I was here. We're not supposed to see each other.

POPPY: And now I'll get told off for running away too. But you were here with me. We're both here but I'm the one who's going to get done. You can just go, but I've got to get told off twice.

PHIL: Poppy, it's not as easy as all that. They said you didn't just kick her. Something else happened. I know this isn't easy, but they're going to ask you about it. That you made her do something she didn't want to do. Something very private.

> *Pause. POPPY turns to go.*

> Poppy, wait…

POPPY: Mrs Sladen will listen to you. She doesn't like mum.

PHIL: How do you know?

POPPY: I can tell. Mum's always complaining about the school.

PHIL: Did you make Jenny do something she didn't want to do, Poppy? Just tell me straight, I'll believe you.

POPPY: It was her idea. She told a lie and I kicked her, but then we made friends. And then she asked me.

PHIL: What?

POPPY: What it felt like.

Pause.

It wasn't for very long. It wasn't my idea.

PHIL: I believe you. *(Pause.)* What was the lie she told? Why did you kick her?

POPPY: She was teasing me saying that I've got two dads. She said you don't bring me to school anymore because I've been naughty. She said I'll have dad number three soon. She's right. Steve keeps coming round... I think he'll be number three.

PHIL: Remember the first time we met? You made me have a game of table football? I remember thinking how grown up you seemed. You let me win.

POPPY: You were rubbish.

PHIL: And then we had a rematch and you let me win again. And I thought... she's going to be a right handful, this one. Real trouble. You never wanted to play girly games.

POPPY: Like what?

PHIL: I dunno. Hopscotch.

POPPY: Are you serious?

PHIL: You don't seem to do what you want to do most of the time. Did you even like me reading *The Hobbit* to you?

POPPY: That's not a boy's book. It's about Bilbo being braver than anyone else thinks he is. I think it'd be better if he was a girl.

PHIL: Give me a hug.

POPPY: Why?

PHIL: Because I think you need one.

POPPY: Why?

PHIL: To make you feel better.

POPPY: I can't.

PHIL: Why not?

POPPY: You left us. You're a stranger. I can't hug strangers.

PHIL: Right.

Pause. POPPY approaches and hugs him. At first he is reluctant, given what she just said, but then embraces her back.

It's gonna be okay. I'll come back to the school with you and we can talk to Mrs Sladen.

She pulls away.

POPPY: You're stupid, Phil.

PHIL: Why?

POPPY: You can't come with me. You can't ever see me again. Mum says if you try to see me she'll get the police.

Lights dim. SARAH enters. After hours at the restaurant.

SPRING 2012. SIX MONTHS PREVIOUSLY.

SARAH: I got home tonight and there was nothing in the fridge. I'm trying to hold down a full-time job and there just isn't enough money… there isn't enough time… there isn't enough of anything anymore. You just walked out and I'm supposed to carry on somehow. We were getting married.

PHIL: Ovens are off.

SARAH: Then you tell me what I'm supposed to do.

PHIL: It's half eleven, Sarah.

SARAH: What does that mean?

PHIL: You could've sorted out some food earlier.

SARAH: Don't you dare judge me, Phil; you don't know what this is like. We're hungry. You tell me what I'm supposed to do with my seven-year-old daughter. She hasn't eaten.

PHIL: *(Quieter.)* What are you doing bringing her here?

SARAH: Don't whisper. She's right there.

PHIL: You can't use her like this.

SARAH: I don't have a choice – we were getting married.

PHIL: Yeah, well, what about my things?

SARAH: What things?

PHIL: You changed the locks.

SARAH: You ran away.

PHIL: With very good reason.

SARAH: What reason, Phil? What reason?

PHIL: I want my things back.

SARAH: So you're bargaining with me now, for some food for my daughter. Is that it?

PHIL: Did you know I'm closing down the restaurant? Of course you did. You turned my staff against me.

SARAH: I didn't do anything.

PHIL: Did you sleep with him? Did you sleep with Steve?

SARAH: I don't know what you're talking about; you're paranoid.

PHIL: Getting your dad to invest in my business. You know I can't get any credit now because of him. That's why I'm closing... because I let you talk me into taking his money. Can't believe how stupid I was. Knew he'd screw me over in the end. He made my name mud in the town. Telling people I'm violent, telling them I beat you up, telling them I'm a vicious drunk. He's like you. Poisonous. Twisted. I can't even walk down the high street without someone making some bullshit comment. Like I'm a leper or something.

Pause. PHIL goes to the bar. From behind it he produces a take-away container.

You know what though; I'm going to be the bigger person. I'm better than all this. There. This is the best I can do. You'll have to heat it up.

SARAH doesn't take it from him. She indicates POPPY. PHIL gives it to POPPY.

There you go. Enjoy.

SARAH: *(Smiling.)* You know it was today, right? You remember that? Our big day. You should've seen the dress... oh, Phil. My arse looked like a million dollars. You could've had me all night long in that dress

She approaches him, but he moves away instinctively.

PHIL: You've kept it, haven't you? Did you put it on this morning? And walk around the house? It'll look better the older you get. That's what happens to you, isn't it? Men propose and then realise at the last minute... like an awakening... hang on... she's a nutter, I can't marry her. And there you'll be, in your fifties with a collection of dresses, wandering round your house late at night, hating yourself for being such a bitch, figuring out if there's enough in the medicine cabinet to do yourself in.

SARAH: He's promised it to me. When you finally stop trying to stay afloat and hand it all over to dad, I'm gonna open this place up. Me and Steve. And we'll make a go of it. Your one big dream and you didn't have the balls to make it work. Didn't have the balls for the real world. We were chatting last night, Poppy and me. Weren't we Pops? And she told me what she really thinks of you now that you're out of our lives. Do you remember Poppy? What you said about Phil? Hey sweetheart.

POPPY exits.

She's scared of you. That's what she told me. That she was always scared of you. Making a child feel like that. I hope you're proud of yourself.

CHRISTMAS 2011. FOUR MONTHS PREVIOUSLY.

A children's play area at night. PHIL has dry blood on his nose.

PHIL: I was sitting on the bed earlier this evening. Poppy was in bed. I turned the TV off and I looked at the clock. It was five past nine. Then I looked out of the window. And I stood there, looking at the street. Then I looked at the clock again and it was ten fourteen. Then I noticed a plastic bag caught high up in the branches of a tree, and I thought to myself 'one day I think I'll go to India'. I remember because I looked at the clock again and it was six minutes to eleven. What time is it now?

LUCY: Nearly two.

PHIL: I don't know what happened between then and now.

LUCY: Tell me

PHIL: I've always had this nagging feeling that I must be stupid. That I don't get it. It's only me who doesn't get it. At school I never quite knew what was expected.

LUCY: Phil...

PHIL: And this thing happens tonight and suddenly she might as well be speaking French. I didn't understand what was going on. Do you remember Miss Hayden? At junior school? Thin woman. Stern. Gave us an assignment once. You won't remember. To write a diary for a week. But I waited for something to write about and nothing happened. So I handed in a blank diary. Because nothing happened. And somehow, that was wrong. Why is that wrong? She couldn't understand why I'd given her seven blank pages. As if one blank page would've been okay. Seven made much more sense to me. It's cold. I kissed you. Do you remember that? You were wearing a turquoise woolly hat. Can we go inside? Please, Lucy. I don't know what to do. I don't know what happened. I don't know.

LUCY: Yes you do. Tell me.

PHIL: I don't know.

LUCY: Phil, you have to talk to me.

PHIL: You don't know what it's like. I can't tell you what happened, I don't know myself. She confuses me, my head's spinning, I can't remember. It's cold. Can we go inside? Please. I don't know what to do.

LUCY: What happened?

PHIL: Let's go to London.

LUCY: No, answer my question, why is Sarah…

PHIL: Come on, let's just go and do something.

LUCY: Why is Sarah covered in blood from a head wound?

PHIL: I've got the car; we could go to St James' Park.

LUCY: The police are looking for you.

PHIL: They won't believe me.

LUCY: What won't they believe?

PHIL: She cracked my head open and kicked me – kept kicking me. And I remember thinking, what's the point of kicking me, you've already cracked my head open? A kick isn't going to do that much damage, not by comparison. It's funny the thoughts you have in the moment.

LUCY: She hit you? With what? Why did she hit you?

PHIL: And then I figured it out. She wasn't kicking me to do damage. It was a status thing. Isn't it funny? Lucy? Isn't it? The thoughts your brain is capable of having even while you're lying there, bleeding on the carpet? A status thing.

LUCY: So she hit you first? Is that what you're saying? Did you hit her back?

PHIL: She called the police and told them I'd attacked her.

LUCY: I've seen her.

PHIL: Why did you go to her?

LUCY: She called me.

PHIL: She did that herself. The head wound.

LUCY: What do you mean she did it herself? She beat herself up?

PHIL: I swear. You've no idea. I watched her. I swear it's true. I watched her trying to crack her own head open. It's true. I didn't touch her. It's insane, but you must believe me. She's done it before. We have these arguments and they go nowhere. Half the time I can't even remember how it started or what the point was, all I know is that she's wrong – she's wrong and it has to stop. She's got to stop because she's being offensive, she's lying, she's rude, she should just SHUT UP, you know, but she keeps lying and insulting me, calling me all sorts and I can't remember why we're arguing what the point was and then BAM. And at first I can't believe it, but then BAM again and I can't believe what I'm seeing and then BAM BAM.

LUCY: Do you hit her, Phil?

PHIL: Lucy, you're not listening. That's not me… that's her hitting her own head against the wall. Again. And again. And maybe that's a status thing too – like she's deliberately trying to destroy both of us.

LUCY: *(Silence.)*

PHIL: Do you believe me?

LUCY: She's making a statement to the police that you attacked her and there's blood coming from her head. I spoke to her… she was calm.

PHIL: It's an act.

LUCY: Calm as anything.

PHIL: She's a professional liar.

LUCY: She told me that you ran away before the police got there.

PHIL: Course I ran; I knew she'd convince them that I was to blame.

LUCY: Phil, she told me you were waiting for her when she came home.

PHIL: I was. She went out for a drink with you and I stayed at home with Poppy.

LUCY: And that when she came home, you were

PHIL: Waiting for her, I was.

LUCY: At the front door.

PHIL: Not at the front door. Well, yes, at the front door, but not outside. I was inside.

LUCY: Waiting for her.

PHIL: I'd been *waiting* for her to come home all night.

LUCY: By the door.

PHIL: Because of the draft excluder. That sausage dog draft excluder. I was pushing it up against the frame when she opened the door. I wasn't sat there all night…

LUCY: Were you angry?

PHIL: No, well, no not really.

LUCY: She said you were angry. Were you angry, Phil?

PHIL: Not straight away.

LUCY: You became angry.

PHIL: She started accusing me.

LUCY: What of?

PHIL: It doesn't make any difference what she was accusing me of. She's got some itch on the inside of her brain and it's got nothing to do with me, but she has to cause a problem to scratch it.

LUCY: What was she accusing you of?

PHIL: Can we go inside; I'm freezing?

LUCY: She's saying you headbutted her. It doesn't matter what you did or didn't do, you can't run away from the police.

PHIL: Not until you tell me you believe me.

LUCY: This is fucked up! Do you promise that you're telling the truth Phil, because right now it's her word against yours?

PHIL: I promise.

LUCY: Then you have to break up with her; you can't continue like this.

PHIL: As of tonight the wedding… the whole thing… it's finally over.

LUCY: You can't avoid this situation.

PHIL: I wasn't trying to… I just needed time to think; had to get my head together. That's why I called you. The police won't believe me; I had to talk to someone who would just let me talk and not judge me. They'll just put me in the back of a car and cart me off to a cell… I needed time to talk. To someone with a friendly face. Someone who trusts me.

She gets out her mobile phone and offers it to him.

LUCY: You have to call them and tell them where you are.

PHIL: Is that what friends are supposed to do, is it? Take sides with someone they barely know just because she's a woman?

LUCY: You ran. You've got guilty written all over you.

PHIL: So that's it.

LUCY: Don't be angry with me, just… Just call them. Okay? We can sort this out.

PHIL: I knew I shouldn't have let you go out with her. She said she wanted to get to know you. My oldest friend. She just wanted to turn you against me. Didn't take long did it?! Nothing like a few drinks down The Feathers and a kebab on the way home to change your mind about someone.

LUCY: No, it wasn't like that…

PHIL: You're the last person I thought would turn their back on me.

LUCY: I believe you. Phil, I believe you.

PHIL: Mean it.

LUCY: Of course I mean it. How can I not? You're my best friend. But the police won't care what I think. You have to call them.

He takes the phone.

CHRISTMAS 2011. EARLIER THE SAME NIGHT.

PHIL is conscious but dazed, bleeding from his nose. SARAH is drunk, unharmed. She holds a bottle. A blood-stained steam iron is on the floor.

SARAH: These guys had wedding rings. They must do that every day of the week. Falling over themselves to buy you drinks. They've probably got kids. One was so blatant about it. Some city boy flashing his money. I could smell coconut and beer. Lucy bought the next round. And I told them to leave us alone.

I try to talk to you. Every day there's something I want to talk to you about. Something I want to – but I get such a bad pain. Here. Today I wanted to tell you. I heard the woman next door crying. I hear her every day. When I see her in the mornings leaving for work she looks so together. In the afternoons she comes home and she cries. There was a beeping noise. I think she was heating something in the microwave and crying and then it was ready and she stopped. And I was about to call you and tell you that I think you're the kindest, loveliest – but my head. Screaming.

We were smoking cigarettes outside the pub and he took me aside to ask me something. Took my arm. And the coconut on his breath was so fresh. And he said to me 'this isn't a whim'. I didn't know what he meant and then he said 'you're getting older' and 'you're getting stronger'. And I didn't know what he meant. And then he took my hand and said 'keep your eyes open, keep your eyes on me'. I couldn't focus, but he took my hand and he was pulling me towards the bench in the market square and he said 'focus on me' but my eyes were closed. And he lifted me onto the bench saying 'you're getting stronger' and I could taste the coconut and beer as he touched me.

I think it must've been hot chocolate. She was heating hot chocolate in the microwave and it was ready and she stopped crying. But then his hands were on me and he was fucking me on the bench and saying 'you're getting

stronger, you're getting better' and my eyes were closed
and I could smell Thai food and then I opened my eyes
and it was your face. Your eyes looking at me. You pushing
your dry shaft burning into me. Your hands pinching
the blood back in my wrists. And I found myself crying
with her, waiting for the hot chocolate but for me it never
came… all over my thighs. And I could only feel it because
by then my eyes were closed. Tight as he breathed out and
twitched.

I look at the wallpaper and those tiny little flowers on the
wallpaper and they seem so far away. I want to smash
through the wall and get one. To feel special. To crawl all
over you. To pinch the blood back in your veins and fuck
you too hard. I want to rape you. Every day I want to rape
you and I'm sorry for it.

And I can picture her with the hot chocolate, that feeling
when you stop crying that maybe you were stupid to have
cried at all, but everything feels just a bit better. And I put
my hand up against the wall and I imagined her doing the
same on the other side and the two of us just touching like
that through the wall… and then I realised that the soft
bit in the middle… the soft of my palm doesn't touch the
wall… and I can't make it touch the wall, even if I push
as hard as I can… the small bit right in the middle… the
softest part… won't touch. And I don't think it's just me.
I don't think she can do it either. And I want to tell you…
I want to tell you that I'm sorry for… all the things… I
know I hurt you. And I want to tell you, but my head is
screaming. And I can't shake it but maybe some beer on
his breath, blowing hot coconut and beer into my face
and he said 'focus on me' and I opened my eyes and there
was Lucy. I tried to tell her. I tried to tell her, but she said
that everything was okay and that I'd been really out of
it… that there's nothing to worry about… that you are the
kindest… that I'm so lucky. That's what she thinks. That
I'm so lucky. And I know she loves you. I know she would
be so much better for you than I could ever be. I'm the

woman next door crying by the microwave. I'm not even here.

I'm sorry, Phil. Please. I'm sorry. I'm sorry. I'm sorry. I'm sorry. I'm sorry.

She moves to the wardrobe and hits her head against it repeatedly with each 'sorry'. He doesn't respond, not because he's dazed, but because he's seen it before. She hits her head harder and harder. As she collapses to the floor he gets up and walks out. She lies motionless on the floor. MICK enters.

SUMMER 2011. FOUR MONTHS PREVIOUSLY.

MICK: And I fainted. Just like that. Stupid, really. Don't you think? Don't you think that was stupid? To work all day long in the sweltering sun, concrete slab after concrete slab, all the cement to mix, just me… in the sweltering heat. Sweltering. In the garden. 'Til I fainted. What do you think?

PHIL is entering. He has no visible wounds, but is utterly exhausted. He brings MICK a cup of tea.

PHIL: I'm not sure what you

MICK: What do you think that says about me, Phil?

PHIL: What it says?

MICK: About me. What do you think that says about a man like me?

PHIL: That you're self-destructive.

MICK: Self-destructive. Would you say that's true? That I'm self-destructive?

PHIL: I don't know, Mick. We've been up all night, I can barely stand.

MICK: Self-destructive.

PHIL: Maybe you are. Maybe you're not. It's not really my concern. I mean, I'm glad you're all right.

MICK: I was dehydrated. Didn't piss for a whole day.

PHIL: I'm just not sure I see the point.

MICK: The point, Phil, is that I used to be… well, I'm sure Sarah's told you a few things. I was a different person when she was growing up.

PHIL: She mentioned one or two

MICK: I mean you may think it's strange. It's okay if you do. It may be strange to you that I'm here. That we're here together. After all, I was the cause of most of the stress, trauma and anxiety in Sarah's young life. I was adulterous, many many times. And I was an angry man.

PHIL: She mentioned those things.

MICK: The point is that the hardest thing to do in life is admit who you are and what you're like. I've done it because I went through counselling. And I was so taken by the whole process that I'm now a counsellor. It does make sense. Don't you think?

PHIL: I just don't see how

SARAH enters with biscuits for MICK. She curls up on him. He strokes her hair.

MICK: That's okay, that's okay. You agreed to talk, that's the main thing. I know you two are in love. You love Sarah? Is love the right word?

PHIL: Yes, but

MICK: But you feel there are things in your relationship that aren't working? There are some changes that need to be made. We can put certain things in place to prevent crisis points developing. So that you both feel like you're being heard. Strategies for coping with different anxieties that surface in difficult ways…

PHIL: You have to understand, Mick... I don't go in for this. I don't need strategies; I don't need to be told how to behave like a human being. That comes... this may sound a little arrogant... but that comes naturally to me. If I need to develop strategies to prevent my partner from losing her mind, then I think I'm better off out of the relationship. Does that make sense to you?

MICK: Well, I have the advantage of knowing my daughter and I know that she is prepared to work hard on this. I mean, she's the kind of person who will literally do whatever it takes. She's been up all night trying to talk you down. You need to be prepared to show the same kind of commitment, but all I can see is yawning and moaning. I mean, this isn't just about you anymore. Poppy has shown a real attachment to you.

PHIL: This is a little bit crazy to me. This whole situation is wrong.

MICK: That's your point of view, that's how you feel, good

PHIL: No, Mick, that's not how I feel, that's not a point of view, that's a cold hard fact. I'm getting out of this relationship because as far as I'm concerned it's completely insane. I'm interested in something, Mick. Can I ask you something?

MICK: Of course... you're letting off steam... that's what I'm here for.

PHIL: Just a hypothetical. What do you do? What's your training? If one partner in counselling tells you they're being physically abused, what do you do?

MICK: If you're saying that you've raised a hand to

PHIL: Okay, that's what I thought. You're not exactly impartial here, are you? Don't worry, that's not what I'm saying. I'm a pacifist, Mick, you don't have to worry about Sarah's safety. This is hypothetical. What do you do? Forget it's me. Forget it's me. It's not Sarah. Okay? She's not being abused. Okay? So there's this hypothetical couple in trouble, they come to you to talk about it and then one of them takes you aside and tells you they're having the shit kicked out of them on a regular basis. What do you do?

MICK: Well, I'm not trained as a

PHIL: I know you're not, Mick. I know that. What do you do?

MICK: I refer them.

PHIL: Who to?

MICK: The relevant organisation

PHIL: Christ, this is like pulling teeth. What organisation?

MICK: Women's Aid or

PHIL: And what if the abused partner is a man?

MICK: Well, there's…

PHIL: Yes?

MICK: Well, that's much less common.

PHIL: So what?

MICK: Well, it doesn't happen.

PHIL: That's not the same thing, Mick. Much less common and doesn't happen… it's not the same.

MICK: What's the problem anyway?

PHIL: What do you mean?

MICK: All a bloke has to do is walk away. Close a door. Leave the room. That's all he has to do.

PHIL: And what if the abuse is psychological.

MICK: What if what?

PHIL: You've never heard of psychological abuse.

MICK: *(Laughing.)* Sorry, Phil, no, sorry, I don't mean to…

PHIL: Last night your daughter accused me…

MICK: I know what you're telling me, Phil. We've been over it a thousand times but Sarah is saying that's not true. You must've got it mixed up, or misheard her. But psychological… I mean, it's all a bit far-fetched, don't you think?

PHIL: This is serious!

SARAH: See?

PHIL: See? What do you mean, 'see'?

SARAH: You're raging. Temper of yours gets in the way of everything.

PHIL: I think I have the right to raise my voice when

MICK: Up to a point, Phil. But it's important that both of you feel safe at all times.

PHIL: Is that right? Feel safe?

MICK: I'll give you a for instance. If a couple gets together and the man… the man, mind you… the man proposes and the woman says yes. Right? And then every two months after she said yes, the man decides he wants the relationship to end. Right? Every two months. That does not develop a sense of security for either partner. Or, for that matter, the woman's daughter by a previous relationship. Does it, Phil? I think that you need to sit down and really think through last night and decide, Phil, what the fuck is important. Because you invest in a relationship, Phil. It's an investment. And you have to look after your investments.

PHIL: I don't know what you're talking about.

MICK: I'm saying, Phil, that men don't leave my daughter. They don't do that. They never have. So I'm thinking that you're struggling. Would I be right in saying that, Phil? Would that be right? Your restaurant isn't doing all that well. And I'm saying that this is causing you stress and that this is why you're considering leaving my daughter. It's understandable.

PHIL: But that's completely beside

MICK: You might think so, Phil, but stress manifests itself in all sorts of ways. Are you stressed, Phil?

PHIL: I run a restaurant

MICK: You run a restaurant, naturally you're stressed. And this stress manifests itself in an irrational

PHIL: Look, there isn't any

MICK: Irrational feelings in the heat of the moment – we're all the same, Phil. We're all the same. Let me help. I can take the stress away.

SARAH: Let him do it, Phil. He wants to.

PHIL: You mean money?

MICK: A helping hand. That's what this family does.

PHIL: You don't want to

MICK: No, Phil, I don't want to. To be honest with you, I prefer Thai food… but that's what this family does. Whatever happened last night is a confused memory…

PHIL: But this is completely… this is beside the point. I'm calling off the engagement; I'm leaving your daughter because

MICK: Of what happened last night. I know. I know, Phil. I know you are. You have a version of last night in your head and it's driving all this anger. But you're not looking at the bigger picture. You're under huge pressure. Both of you. Let me help. Okay? Imagine not having to worry about the finances. Imagine that.

PHIL: Last night, she accused me of

MICK: There's a lot of this and that, Phil. In all situations like this it gets heated and people say things or don't say things. It's confusing and it can be hard to remember what actually happened. Look, it doesn't matter who I believe, Phil. I'm not relevant here. We can get into who said what, but that way it'll never end. Just see this for what it is. You love each other very much. Everyone can see that. I'm her father. All right? We can get through this. I'll be a totally silent partner. All right? All right?

PHIL: You know, there's one thing I can't understand. I see it in your face; just the same way I see it in hers. You're talking to me. I can see your lips moving, I can hear your words. But there's absolutely no flicker of recognition. Do you know what I mean by that, Mick? You could be talking to me, to a a a dog or a bloody sofa… there's nothing in your eyes that's got anything to do with me. This is all about you. And I don't know, because it's not there, I don't know how much you realise how serious last night was. I know you know it, because I told you, but I can't see it anywhere in your face. The lie is perfect. And it terrifies me.

MICK: You're wound up tighter than a spring. You need my help, Phil. Just let me. I'm happy to. Or you can leave. It's up to you Phil, it has to be your decision. You can leave right now, or we can sort this out like adults.

PHIL is exhausted and his strength leaves him as MICK embraces him.

SUMMER 2011. THE PREVIOUS NIGHT.

PHIL stands outside the bathroom. The door is locked with SARAH inside.

PHIL: Sarah, we have to get to the bottom of this.

SARAH: *(Off.)* You have to go now. Have to go now.

PHIL: *(Angry.)* Sarah!

SARAH: *(Off.)* Not letting you in.

PHIL: Sarah, that's fine. I don't need to come in. I need you to talk to me. Something very serious happened and we need to talk. I need you to see reason.

SARAH: *(Off. Suddenly soft.)* Phil, what happened?

PHIL: I'm not sure, babe. That's what I want to find out. We had a lovely day, didn't we?

SARAH: *(Off. Agreeing.)* Mm.

PHIL: We went to your dad's for the barbecue. Poppy played with the neighbour's boys. We all had too much to eat and lazed around in the garden.

SARAH: *(Off. Quietly.)* You played swing ball with Poppy.

PHIL: What was that, sweetheart?

SARAH: *(Off.)* Swingball with Poppy.

PHIL: Yes, swingball. And you were chatting to the neighbours… Tom and… Karen.

SARAH: *(Off.)* Catherine.

PHIL: Catherine, that's right. And we listened to some music.

SARAH: *(Off.)* You played guitar.

PHIL: Yes, we got the guitar out. Then Poppy said she wanted to sleep over, so I came back to get some things for her. Then we left Poppy and we went to the pub with Tom and Karen. Catherine. Playing pool, having a laugh. And we came home. You didn't want to go to bed, so… we were dancing.

SARAH: *(Off.)* No.

PHIL: Yes, we were dancing. The stereo was on, we'd had a lot of wine and we were dancing in the living room.

SARAH: *(Off.)* You were.

PHIL: Then we got tired and went up to bed. You undressed me.

SARAH: *(Off.)* No.

PHIL: Sarah, you looked at me. You looked at me and you smiled and, yes, you started with the shirt and you slowly undressed me.

SARAH: *(Off.)* I didn't.

PHIL: Sarah, I want us both to know exactly what happened. I can't let this become something else later on. You unzipped me. You took my trousers down...

SARAH: *(Off.)* You forced me.

PHIL: No! Sarah, no! You can't say that. You mustn't say that. I want you to understand you can't say that. Do not say that. It's not right. It's a lie. It's a lie, Sarah. You're lying now. We both know that. You're lying and we both know. You took my trousers down and you started to

SARAH: *(Off.)* Phil, stop... please...

PHIL: Sarah, this is important. We have to understand what happened. You can't lie about this.

SARAH: *(Off.)* Not lying!

PHIL: You are! You took my trousers down and you sucked me off.

SARAH: *(Off.)* Leave me alone!

PHIL: This is all a performance Sarah, you know it and I know it. You have to stop performing. And then I laid you back on the bed and we had... we made love, Sarah, don't you remember? You must remember. Please try to remember, Sarah. We had sex.

SARAH: *(Off.)* No, no, no, no.

PHIL: It was just sex.

SARAH: *(Off.)* No, no, no, no.

PHIL: Sarah, listen to me. I. Did. Not. Rape. You.

She cries quietly.

We need to be very clear about this, okay? We had sex. You're my fiancé; I have absolutely no reason to rape you. Do I? Would I do something like that?

SARAH: *(Off.)* No.

PHIL: No, I wouldn't, that's right. You're just very, very drunk. You got it wrong. Okay?

SARAH: *(Off.)* I was there.

PHIL: You were there in body, but you were very, very drunk. You hardly knew what my name was.

SARAH: *(Off.)* Isn't that rape?

PHIL: No. No. No. It's not… rape, Sarah. Okay? Okay? Okay?

She starts to shiver. Long pause.

I think we need to talk about this in the morning. I hope you think about the impact this could have on me if it stays like that in your mind.

SARAH: *(Off.)* Where are you going?

PHIL: Bed.

SARAH: *(Off.)* I'll sleep downstairs.

PHIL: You're not scared of me, Sarah. You're not scared of me. This is all a performance.

SARAH: *(Off.)* You don't know how I feel.

PHIL: You're pretending.

Long pause. Silence.

SARAH: *(Off.)* Phil? Phil? *(To herself.)* Oh God. Don't go.

She gathers herself, unlocks the door and leaves the toilet as quickly as she can. She is immediately pushed against the wall by PHIL. He is quietly seething. His movements are not sudden or violent, but

extremely steady and very forceful. He pushes her up against the wall.
He holds her by her shoulders.

PHIL: Say it.

SARAH: Say what?

PHIL: I need to hear you say it.

SARAH: Say what?

PHIL: I am not a rapist.

SARAH: Phil, you're hurting.

PHIL: I'm not hurting you, Sarah. I'm not hurting you, this is
    controlled. I need you to say it. Say it, Sarah, I need you to
    admit you're lying. I need you to say it. Say it. Say it.

SARAH: I'm frightened.

PHIL: No, you're not. You know I'm not going to hurt you
    because I'm not a violent man and I'm not a rapist. Say it,
    Sarah.

SARAH: You can't expect me like this

PHIL: *(Screams.)* Say it!

SARAH: Phil, I need you to let go of me.

Long pause. Very slowly, he lets go and backs away.

PHIL: Say it.

SARAH slowly moves away from him. Long pause.

PHIL: Why do you do this?

She moves slowly up to him and puts her arms around his waist from
behind. Pause. Slowly he turns and embraces her. Pause.

SARAH: *(Quietly.)* Catherine.

PHIL: What?

SARAH: It's Catherine. You pretended not to know her name,
    but you know exactly what her name is.

PHIL: What are you talking about?

SARAH: I saw you all afternoon. She wanted you and you wanted her. I could see it in your eyes. And you raped me because you couldn't have it. Didn't you. Didn't you Phil?

She begins to kiss him, very tenderly. He is bewildered, disorientated and unable to respond. She continues to kiss him.

And I forgive you. Phil. I forgive you, because I love you so much.

SPRING 2011. THREE MONTHS EARLIER.

POPPY: Did everyone ride on horses?

PHIL: I'm not that old.

POPPY: I bet they did.

PHIL: I was seven in the eighties, not the middle ages.

POPPY: I bet you did cave paintings.

PHIL: Cheeky little madam. *(Grandly.)* I had a Sinclair Spectrum 48K when I was seven. That's a computer.

POPPY: I bet the internet was really slow back then.

PHIL: *(Smiling to himself, not wanting to tell her the truth.)* Yeah… yeah, really slow. There's one thing I remember clearly from being seven. My dad used to read every night. Sat in a chair by the bed with his big feet next to mine. Or he'd lay down next to me and I'd keep rolling towards him, trying not to get stuck under his back. And he'd read all about Bilbo Baggins and Gandalf and Thorin. And I remember at the time he'd keep stopping. I'd have to beg him to keep going. I thought he was bored or he'd fallen asleep or something, but he just stopped reading out loud because he got so engrossed in the story. Reading quietly to himself. That's how I knew it meant just as much to him as it did to me… he'd only read stories he loved himself. Ones that would carry him away. Really sharing something.

POPPY: We used to have a cat called Tuppence. Dad used to make up stories about where Tuppence had been at night. The trouble she used to get into with the neighbours cats and the hedgehogs in the garden. He pretended they were true. I pretended to believe them.

PHIL: I didn't have to pretend to believe in hobbits. Everyone knows they're real.

POPPY: They are not.

PHIL: Ah, that's what I said at first. The thing I always loved about hobbits... wherever they went, however remote they were, however cold and wet, they could always light a fire and it always seemed to remind Bilbo of home.

POPPY: Who's Bilbo?

PHIL: I can introduce you.

POPPY: I have to go to bed.

PHIL: You sure?

POPPY: Tuppence got run over. I found her in the street in front of our house. All her insides coming out. Dad stopped telling stories after that. I wanted him to, but he said I wouldn't believe them. I touched her insides with my finger.

SARAH has entered without either of them noticing.

SARAH: Why aren't you in bed?

POPPY: I couldn't sleep.

SARAH: Can't you take her up?

PHIL: We were just talking.

SARAH: Yeah, I heard. Steve came to the restaurant.

POPPY: Who's Steve?

SARAH: Why didn't you tell me?

PHIL: Haven't had chance, we've both been so busy.

POPPY: Who's Steve?

SARAH: No one love. Why didn't you ask me?

PHIL: I'm sorry?

SARAH: He's a slimy… Phil, you can't take him on.

POPPY: Why's he slimy?

PHIL: He is not.

SARAH: He virtually… Poppy go upstairs please.

POPPY: What? He virtually what?

SARAH: He came onto me.

PHIL: Steve? I think you read that wrong. Don't worry about it.

SARAH: Why would I lie? He told me all about what happened with you and his ex-fiancé.

PHIL: That? They weren't engaged, that was years ago. I can barely remember that. What did he say?

SARAH: He said it… Poppy can you please go up to bed?

POPPY: Come with me.

SARAH: I will, in a minute darling. Phil, can you please take this seriously? I'm not comfortable with him working for us.

PHIL: For me.

SARAH: What?

PHIL: It's my restaurant, you don't do hiring and firing.

SARAH: Where did that come from?

PHIL: I knew you'd react like this. You hate it when I make a decision without consulting you, but it's my business and I'll do whatever I like.

POPPY: Read me a story Phil.

PHIL: Not now, mum's coming up with you.

SARAH: I'm telling you he made some inappropriate comments and he touched me.

PHIL: Oh, he touched you now? So your story changed in the last thirty seconds, how convenient when you're not in control of a situation. That's how it works, isn't it?

SARAH: Phil, please.

PHIL: You're making a mountain out of a molehill. You don't know what you're talking about. You got him wrong. Steve stays.

SARAH: I don't know what I'm talking about?

PHIL: No, you haven't got a clue.

SARAH: Don't patronise me, Phil.

PHIL: I'm not; you actually don't know what you're talking about. Steve's a great chef.

POPPY: Who's Steve?

SARAH: Who clearly thinks he's more important than me.

PHIL: He is.

SARAH: What?

PHIL: He's the bloody chef, he's more important than anyone.

SARAH: Why are you being like this? Why's your mate suddenly so important?

PHIL: It's got nothing to do with Steve. You're not in charge; that's the point.

SARAH: I'm not trying to

PHIL: Yes, you are.

SARAH: You invited me to be a part of the business; I'm only looking out for you.

PHIL: Yeah, I gave you a job, but you've got no right to control the decisions I make…

SARAH: Why does it have to come back to control? You're so paranoid.

POPPY: Mum.

PHIL: Am I? You changed next week's rota so I'm always working the same shifts as you. I'm trying to be patient with you, but it feels like I'm in a cage half the time.

SARAH: I want to work with my partner, what's wrong with that?

PHIL: You want to keep an eye on me because you don't trust me, more like. What about Poppy? How're we going to managed childcare?

POPPY: Mum!

SARAH: My dad said he'd help.

PHIL: Not exactly best solution for Poppy, is it?

SARAH: What's wrong with my dad?

PHIL: Plenty, from what you've told me.

SARAH: You can't criticise the way he looks after Poppy and anyway, I don't have to justify my decisions to you, Poppy's perfectly

PHIL: I'm getting tired of this, Sarah. Every time I do something without consulting you, this happens. It's not normal. This is not a normal relationship. I know I promised to be patient with you, but it's getting so frustrating, I can't even make a business decision now without you getting…

SARAH: Don't shout.

PHIL: *(Shouting.)* Why do you always say that? I'm not shouting.

POPPY drops her glass. It smashes on the floor.

SARAH: Come on, luv. Phil's getting angry again. We'll let him clear that up.

SARAH and POPPY exit.

SPRING 2011. ONE MONTH EARLIER.

The restaurant. It is closed, but set up for the big opening.

SARAH: I said what do you think?

PHIL: *(Off.)* What do I think? I can't really have an opinion, can I?

SARAH: Why not?

PHIL: *(Off.)* I'm an atheist.

SARAH: Listen to you. Fuckin' hell, I'm only talking. *(Mock voice.)* I'm an atheist. Like that makes you God or something.

PHIL: *(Off.)* Ha!

SARAH: Everyone can have an idea of what heaven's like.

PHIL: *(Off.)* Sounds great.

SARAH: Is that it?

PHIL: *(Entering half-dressed in chef whites.)* What do you want me to say?

SARAH: Oh, Phil, don't be like that. I'm just talking.

PHIL: You're never just talking.

SARAH: Don't let's…

PHIL: It's all right, I'm not… I'm not… look, it sounds great.

SARAH: You already said that.

PHIL: But it does. It sounds… heavenly.

SARAH: If you're going to take the piss.

PHIL: Okay, okay… I think I mean… I mean… we deserve
somewhere like that.

SARAH: Do we?

PHIL: Of course. Only the best.

She hugs him. Then presses her forehead against his.

SARAH: Then just let it be there in your mind.

PHIL: I can't.

SARAH: Phil… Phil… stop talking. Just allow it.

PHIL: I am an atheist; you can't expect me to believe in your
vision of what heaven might be. Lovely as it sounds. A
series of ponds with a waterfall. Heaven, great. But it's your
heaven. Now can we please get ready?

SARAH: What about Poppy?

PHIL: What about her?

SARAH: Thanks a lot; I'm sure she'd love to hear you say that.

PHIL: No… no… please understand. When I die, I'm going
to rot. My soul won't go anywhere. Poppy can believe
whatever she wants, so can you… if she wants to imagine
the three of us will be up there, or whatever, in the end,
then that's fine. I don't.

SARAH: Have you got any idea how upsetting that is?

PHIL: I can't do anything about it, Sarah. I don't believe in
God.

SARAH: What do you believe in?

PHIL: Why, when we've only got an hour to get my first
restaurant open to the public, are you so desperate to talk

about heaven? It's not as though it takes much imagination. A waterfall? Are you joking? That's the oldest cliché in the book. I suppose Bob Marley's there smoking a joint singing 'every little thing's gonna be alright'.

SARAH: It's at times like this I realise how much you're going to let me down.

PHIL: *(Laughs.)* Are you serious?

SARAH: Don't laugh at me, Phil. I've left Poppy with dad because your restaurant is too pompous for children, I mean; she's six she's not a baby. I'm here all on my own running the bar and greeting your customers and all I want… all I want is a bit of support.

PHIL: Babe, don't cry. You're not on your own. I'm here, look.

SARAH: You don't give a shit about me.

PHIL: Come here.

He tries to give her a hug. As he does so, she shrugs him off, but with a slap to his face. A pause.

Ow.

Pause.

Sarah.

Pause. She slaps his other cheek, but not as hard and with a smile. Pause. He smiles too.

Bitch.

SARAH: What did you call me?

PHIL: Bitch.

SARAH: No one talks to me like that.

He makes a grab for her. She is quicker and evades him. They laugh. He picks her up. He supports her and lets her kiss his neck.

I'm starving, Phil. I'll eat you up before the customers get here and run this place on my own with you inside me. Starting with your neck. This is a beautiful neck.

She kisses his neck gently.

PHIL: Why are you with me? You're so beautiful. Way out of my league.

SARAH: *(Smiling.)* Don't be silly.

PHIL: I mean it. You're the one they look at.

SARAH: Who?

PHIL: People. You're the one in the restaurant people are aware of. You smile at men and it makes them self-conscious. I'm not in that league. I don't mind not being in that league, but I'm definitely not. I never have been.

SARAH: Phil, this body, your face, everything about you is perfect.

PHIL: Hardly…

SARAH: It's about what I see.

She kisses his face and shoulders. She gets down from his arms and caresses his torso. She slowly, gently dresses him, taking pride in every fold of his clothes and every contour of his body. It has an erotic charge, but more than this, an affection, genuine love and admiration.

You do things because they mean something to you. I'd love to be inside your head, to know what it's like to see the world the way you do. To feel things like you do. I've thought about tonight so many times. Coming in and out of the kitchen and we're both calm – busy, but not rushed. It's all within us. And we smile and joke as people are slowly wowed. And I chat to the customers, telling them all about your vision for the place and all the things you want to do with it and I'm just a messenger really, I'm just watching it all, even though I'm involved, I'm watching you make all these people happy. And at the end of the night you come out from the kitchen and everyone looks at you. Me included, we all just watch as you enter the room and everyone applauds and I kiss you and you put your hand in the small of my back and it's all for you, all the smiles and congratulations, but I'm there by your side, as your girlfriend and in that moment everyone can see we'd do anything for each other.

She has dressed him. She kisses him.

PHIL: I need to marry you.

They look at each other. At first she doesn't believe him, but then realises he's serious. She backs away, frightened. She turns and leaves the restaurant. PHIL follows. Pause. LUCY enters. PHIL returns. He embraces her.

PHIL: Oh my God! You're not here. You're travelling.

LUCY: My head's still in India, I think. I came home early. It's so good to see you; I missed you Phil.

PHIL: You too. What happened?

LUCY: You started a restaurant.

PHIL: No, I mean in India. Your gap year.

LUCY: I know what you mean, dummy. India's incredible. I'll tell you all about it as we go, I'm here to help.

PHIL: You came home for this?

LUCY: Phil, you couldn't organise a piss up in a brewery, there must be shitloads still to do. Stop wasting time. Here.

She gives him an iPod.

Playlist. Background music. No clichés, no jazz

BOTH: … no Dean bloody Martin.

PHIL: You made me a mix tape.

LUCY: You always did them for me. There's no Radiohead on there though; don't want any suicides before the main course.

PHIL: And what if I've already sorted the music out?

LUCY: You haven't; you've forgotten.

He concedes that she's right.

PHIL: Thanks.

LUCY: What can I do?

PHIL: Napkins, menus, champagne flutes are still in boxes, there's a wall light still not working and I've run out of butter.

LUCY: You're a bloody nightmare.

They get busy.

PHIL: So, come on. Stories. What was it like?

LUCY: People always talk about the scale of the place, but it really is unbelievable. You've never seen so many people in your life. Mumbai was like another planet.

PHIL: You must've met some cool people.

LUCY: Yeah, one or two. *(Pause.)* Not a patch on Moneypenny though.

PHIL: Eh?

LUCY: Thought you must've joined MI6 the last few months. No one's heard from you. No Facebook, no emails… figured you were On Her Majesty's Secret Service, incognito.

PHIL: Oh, yeah, well my computer's been playing up…

LUCY: You've got an iPhone.

PHIL: Sorry, I've been busy, y'know. This place. Everything. What?

LUCY: Nothing, I just… I was missing home a bit. Would've been nice to see a friendly face. We said we'd Skype each other.

PHIL: You? Missing home? I didn't expect to hear anything at all once you left. The world didn't know what it was letting itself in for. Remember I said to you

LUCY: Because I met someone. A guy.

PHIL: Really?! Tell me more! I was starting to think you might be a lesbian.

LUCY: Well, there's a thought.

PHIL: British?

LUCY: Aussie. Working as a lifeguard.

PHIL: Wow, great. So what happened?

LUCY: It was just like you imagine. We were on a beach. A load of different nationalities. All getting drunk. And we got chatting. He had a tattoo on his arm of a prawn, which I tortured him endlessly about all night.

PHIL: A prawn?

LUCY: Because he wanted to be a chef.

PHIL: You liked him.

LUCY: And he stayed in my tent. He kept talking about his plans and I was telling him about this place and you and, I think, in the end we talked so long we fell asleep in the middle of a sentence.

PHIL: Did you bring this guy home to get hitched, or something? Is that why you're back?

LUCY: No, he took everything.

PHIL: What do you mean?

LUCY: The next day he'd taken my bag and my phone. I was upset and I had mum on the phone getting hysterical and I realised, actually, that all I really wanted was to tell you about it. So I called... and then I emailed. Facebook. Twitter. Nothing. And so I got on a plane because I had nothing left and all I could do was come home and tell you about it in person. Now. And to say to you that I think it was significant that you were the person I wanted to talk to first. And to say that I think I've been getting you and me a little bit wrong. And I think you have too. And that I think I'd like to put that right. And I didn't mean to say all that because this is the wrong time.

SARAH has re-entered.

PHIL: Lucy, this is… Sarah.

LUCY: Sarah, hi.

PHIL: My…

SARAH: His fiancée.

LUCY: Wow, fiancée. Phil! You didn't… I go away for six months and…

PHIL: It's been a bit of a whirlwind.

There is a long pause.

LUCY: Congratulations sweetheart. I can't believe you didn't tell me. *(She hugs him.)* That's… that's very quick.

PHIL: I know. It's great.

LUCY: I mean… yes, great. How wonderful.

SARAH: Thank you.

LUCY: We went to school together. I'm sure he's told… congratulations! Actually, I came to help. With the grand opening. Exciting, isn't it?

SARAH: Yes, very. I'm front of house. It's all organised.

LUCY: Oh god, yes, of course. I'm sure it is. I can serve drinks if you like. Welcome people in. Wash glasses.

SARAH: It's a small place. We don't really have any staff.

LUCY: Oh, I don't want a job. Just to help.

PHIL: You can be a guest, if you like. You'll know people.

SARAH: You said there wasn't any extra room.

LUCY: It's okay. I don't want to be in the way.

PHIL: Really, it's not a problem.

LUCY: No, Phil. Thanks. *(Pause. She moves to the door.)* You didn't reply. You should've e-mailed back.

Pause. She leaves.

PHIL: Old friend.

SARAH: Sorry, I was rude to her. And I'm sorry for running off. Just needed a minute. Listen, the religion thing, the idea of heaven. I get it. It's funny to you because it's all a big fantasy, like Father Christmas. Please, let me finish. I had to have something like that because my parents were so destructive. I don't want pity. But Father Christmas in my house used to come in on Christmas Eve and kick the shit out of mum. So she left. And I didn't go with her because I honestly couldn't decide who was worse. See, she'd wait until he was asleep before she retaliated. And anyway I couldn't go with her because I ended up in care. It's not a sob story, I promise, you just need to know because sometimes there are things I find difficult. I came back to say sorry. I get scared sometimes. The restaurant, people… you. It's not really something I know how to control. But I'm really working hard at it. And I hope that's okay.

PHIL: You don't need to worry about Lucy, she's really…

SARAH: Let's just take one thing at a time. I don't know what that was about, but it sounded far too big for me to handle right now. Maybe, for a little while, if it's okay, you don't try to spend too much time with her. I'll be okay with it eventually, I just need time. For now, let's just focus on tonight. Please. As a couple. Engaged.

ONE MONTH EARLIER.

PHIL stands in SARAH's doorway. She is in a dressing gown.

SARAH: You can't come in. Not that you *can't*, you just can't.

PHIL: I know. It's okay.

SARAH: You can't just text me.

PHIL: Why not?

SARAH: To say you're at the front door? You can't do that. You have to go.

PHIL: I was thinking about earlier.

SARAH: Seriously, please…

PHIL: When I walked you to the door, I didn't kiss you and I've been thinking about not kissing you ever since and I realised that…

SARAH: It was the right thing to do.

PHIL: Was it?

SARAH: Of course it was. Please go.

PHIL: So I came to tell you that, on reflection, not kissing you was the best decision I've made in a long time. Definitely.

SARAH: You woke me up at two in the morning for that? You're lucky my phone was on silent.

PHIL: Also… I bought you a present.

He gives her a small box.

But don't open it.

SARAH: Phil… you're not listening. Poppy's dad's here. Inside. In bed. With me.

PHIL: No, you're standing here.

SARAH: Don't. Please.

PHIL: You said it was over. To me, you said that to me.

SARAH: It is. Really, thank you. But I can't.

She wants to give the box back. He refuses to take it.

PHIL: Wait, just wait. Open it. It's a set of teaspoons. Six. Because it's really late and everything's closed except Tesco and they had flowers, but I thought your daughter might be suspicious tomorrow when she saw them. You don't want her to know about me yet. I get that. I could've bought food but I need to do that properly at some point, for you, if, you know, if you'd like that because I'm an excellent cook, did I tell you I'm going to open a restaurant? And I'll cook for you there if, you know, I'm not assuming that you'll necessarily want to see me again or anything, and you can be my official vegetarian advisor because all vegetarians are freaks and I need someone to...

SARAH: Are you saying I'm a freak?

PHIL: ...so that leaves toilet duck, Adam Sandler movies, charcoal and antacid tablets. So, obviously, I bought you some teaspoons.

She has opened the box to confirm. It is full of teaspoons. She looks at him.

If it's over why did you meet me for dinner?

SARAH: He babysat tonight. I let him stay. He doesn't know I was on a...

PHIL: A date. You can say it. It was definitely a date.

SARAH: Do I look like a girl who doesn't own teaspoons?

PHIL: No.

SARAH: Did you buy them for yourself and pretend they're for me?

PHIL: You have to look beyond the spoon. The point is the effect of the spoon.

SARAH: The effect of the spoon.

PHIL: There. It's happened already. You feel that?

SARAH: Has this worked before? Because…

PHIL: I figured it out tonight. When you let me order your meal.

SARAH: And what did that tell you?

PHIL: That you're feeling trapped, isolated and that you need someone to come along and liberate you.

SARAH: Liberate? With a set of spoons? This isn't Colditz. And what if I told you that I let you order for me as a test?

PHIL: A test of what?

SARAH: To see how decisive you are.

PHIL: So me choosing the mushroom risotto told you…?

SARAH: Nothing. But you didn't check with me first, just gave my order straight to the waitress.

PHIL: I know the restaurant; they do a mean risotto.

SARAH: You knew you were right.

PHIL: So I'm confident.

SARAH: Arrogant.

PHIL: Trusting that if I was wrong we could send the risotto back.

SARAH: And you gave that waitress every last bit of your attention. She blushed.

PHIL: Just being polite.

SARAH: Seductive. You're a big challenge for me.

PHIL: Why do you say that?

SARAH: Because you're not as nice as you think you are. And I just might be the person to show that to you. And I don't want you to hate me for it.

PHIL: The teaspoons… were an innocent thing. A joke.

SARAH: You knew you were being charming.

PHIL: At least I didn't try to fork you on our first date. Sorry, that was… have I done the wrong thing, coming here?

SARAH: Yes.

PHIL: Does he… is it over between you two?

SARAH: Yes, of course it is.

PHIL: It's not, is it?

SARAH: That's what I'm talking about. You know it's not. And yet here you are.

PHIL: Here I am.

SARAH: Not as nice as you think you are. Whatever we do… whatever happens… from this point on… we're both to blame.

PHIL: In that case, for whatever I'm about to do, I'm really sorry.

SARAH: I'm sorry too.

They kiss.

End.

www.ingramcontent.com/pod-product-compliance
Ingram Content Group UK Ltd.
Pitfield, Milton Keynes, MK11 3LW, UK
UKHW020727280225
455688UK00012B/539